Simone Biles

Gold Medal Gymnast and Advocate for Healthy Living

Kylie Burns

Crabtree Publishing Company

www.crabtreebooks.com

Author: Kylie Burns

Series research and development: Reagan Miller

Editorial director: Kathy Middleton

Editor: Ellen Rodger

Proofreader: Wendy Scavuzzo

Photo researcher: Samara Parent

Designer and prepress technician: Samara Parent

Print coordinator: Katherine Berti

Photographs:

Alamy: © MediaPunch Inc: page 23

AP Photo: © Chris Pizzello/Invision/AP: title page; © Ron Sachs/picture-alliance/dpa: page 6; © Matthias Schrader: pages 8-9; © Dmitri Lovetsky: pages 10, 12, 30; © Elise Amendola: pages 14-15; © Melissa J. Perenson/CSM: page 16; © Michael Ciaglo/Houston Chronicle: page 22; © Charles Sykes: pages 24-25; © Paul Ladd /Invision for Kellogg Company: page 26; © LM Otero: page 28

Getty Images: © Laurence Griffiths: pages 4-5; © Kohjiro Kinno /Sports Illustrated: page 7; © THOMAS COEX/AFP: page 19; © Jean Catuffe: pages 20-21; © Eric McCandless/ABC: page 27

Keystone Press: © David Drufke/ZUMA: page 13; © Melissa J. Perenson/CSM: page 17; © Enrico Calderoni/Aflo Sport: page 18

Shutterstock.com: © Petr Toman: cover; © Leonard Zhukovsky: page 11 (all); © Kathy Hutchins: page 29

All other images from Shutterstock

Library and Archives Canada Cataloguing in Publication

Burns, Kylie, author
     Simone Biles : gold medal gymnast and advocate for healthy living / Kylie Burns.

(Remarkable lives revealed)
Includes index.
Issued in print and electronic formats.
ISBN 978-0-7787-4701-7 (hardcover).--
ISBN 978-0-7787-4712-3 (softcover).--
ISBN 978-1-4271-2074-8 (HTML)

     1. Biles, Simone, 1997- --Juvenile literature. 2. Women gymnasts--United States--Biography--Juvenile literature. 3. Gymnasts--United States--Biography--Juvenile literature. I. Title. II. Series: Remarkable lives revealed

GV460.2.B55B87 2018   j796.44092   C2017-907722-8
                                                            C2017-907723-6

Library of Congress Cataloging-in-Publication Data

Names: Burns, Kylie, author.
Title: Simone Biles : gold medal gymnast and advocate for healthy livi / Kylie Burns.
Description: New York, New York : Crabtree Publishing Company, 20 |Series: Remarkable lives revealed | Includes index. | Audience: Age 7-10. | Audience: Grade 4 to 6.
Identifiers: LCCN 2017057534 (print) | LCCN 2017059303 (ebook) | ISBN 9781427120748 (Electronic HTML) | ISBN 9780778747017 (reinforced library binding : alk. paper) | ISBN 9780778747123 (pbk. : alk. paper)
Subjects: LCSH: Biles, Simone, 1997---Juvenile literature. | Gymnasts -United States--Biography--Juvenile literature. | Women gymnasts-United States--Biography--Juvenile literature.
Classification: LCC GV460.2.B55 (ebook) | LCC GV460.2.B55 B87 2018 (print) | DDC 796.44092 [B] --dc23
LC record available at https://lccn.loc.gov/2017057534

Crabtree Publishing Company

www.crabtreebooks.com   1-800-387-7650

Printed in the U.S.A./032018/BG20180202

Published in Canada
Crabtree Publishing
616 Welland Ave.
St. Catharines, Ontario
L2M 5V6

Published inthe United States
Crabtree Publishing
PMB 59051
350 Fifth Ave., 59th Floor
New York, NY 10118

Published in theUnited Kingdom
Crabtree Publishing
Maritime House
Basin Road North, Hove
BN41 1WR

Published in Australia
Crabtree Publishing
3 Charles Street
Coburg North
VIC, 3058

Contents

Perseverance and Positivity

Every person has a different life story. Some people are famous. Others aren't widely known. But everyone has remarkable qualities. **Perseverance** and **positivity** are two qualities that make champion Olympic gymnast Simone Biles remarkable. As a young child, she had to persevere through a difficult family situation. As an elite athlete, she kept a positive attitude even when others made fun of her or when she failed to do her best. With determination and a positive outlook, she learned to live with the challenges in her life. As she grew older, she worked hard to become the best gymnast she could be. Today, pluck and persistence have made her dreams come true. Simone Biles' amazing accomplishments inspire people all over the world.

What Is a Biography?

A biography is the story of a person's life and experiences. We read biographies to learn about another person's life. A biography is based on primary sources, such as a person's own words or pictures, and secondary sources such as information from friends, family, media, and research.

Simone Biles has won more Olympic medals than any other American gymnast.

Remarkable Simone

During a trip to a gymnastics club when Simone was just 6 years old, one of the coaches at the club noticed how Simone copied the skills of the older gymnasts. Simone was determined to learn more, so she asked her family to enroll her in gymnastics lessons. That was the beginning of Simone's incredible journey to becoming a world-famous Olympic athlete. As you read about Simone Biles, think about the qualities that made her achievements possible.

? THINK ABOUT IT

How do you define remarkable? Do you know any remarkable people? What qualities do they have?

Early Struggles

Simone Arianne Biles was born on March 14, 1997, in Columbus, Ohio. She has an older sister and brother, Ashley and Tevin, and a younger sister, Adria. Life at home was difficult. Simone and her siblings were often sent to live in **foster care** when they were young. Simone's mother was in and out of jail due to her addiction to drugs and alcohol. She was often not able to care for her children. Simone's father was not part of their lives. Her grandparents decided to adopt Simone and Adria even though they already had two teenage sons at the time. They became her mom and dad. Simone's older sister and brother were adopted by another member of the family.

Simone has achieved a lot in her life. Her accomplishments have made her a role model. Here, she presents President Barack Obama and first lady Michelle with a surfboard on behalf of the 2016 Olympic team.

A Spring in Her Steps

Simone grew up in Spring, Texas, near Houston. Spring has a population of about 54,000 people. Simone was such an active child that her family once caught her doing backflips off the mailbox! As a young athlete, Simone was required to train for hours each day. She missed a lot of school and school activities. The intense training schedule meant that Simone had to be **homeschooled** for high school. She earned her high school diploma in 2015.

Training is hard work. Simone trains about 32 hours a week at the gym.

Natural Talent

After her first year in gymnastics lessons, Simone showed a lot of talent and skill. She advanced quickly with the help of her coach, Aimee Boorman. They had a strong bond, and Aimee's kind but firm approach encouraged Simone to keep pushing herself. Aimee understood how to motivate Simone and spent many hours with her every day. Simone often referred to her coach as her "second mom." With Aimee's guidance, she attended her first Junior National competition in 2012 at the age of 15. Under Olympic rules, gymnasts have to be at least 16 to compete in the Olympics. Simone was too young to qualify for the 2012 Olympics. She set her sights on the 2016 games instead.

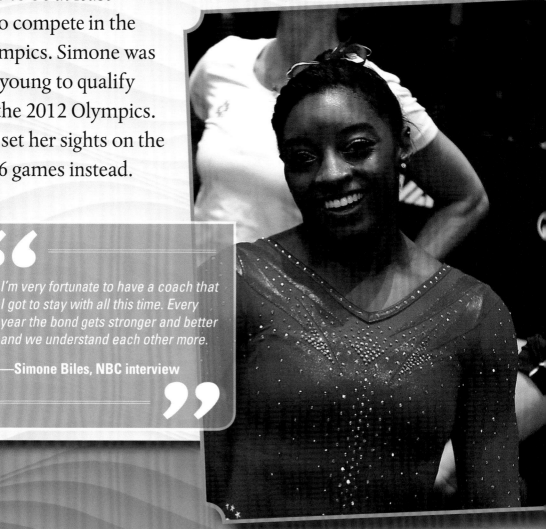

> "I'm very fortunate to have a coach that I got to stay with all this time. Every year the bond gets stronger and better and we understand each other more.
>
> —Simone Biles, NBC interview

More Work, Less Play

The next four years involved the most intense training of Simone's life. She made many sacrifices so she could train. She missed out on ordinary teenage experiences such as dances, eating junk food, and staying up late. Being healthy and strong was key for achieving her dream of becoming an Olympic athlete. Simone kept going and stayed focused every day. She also spent time running and swimming as part of her cross-training exercises.

? THINK ABOUT IT

Imagine that you had to choose between focusing on your sport for hours a day, or going to school with your friends. Would it be an easy choice? What do you think helped Simone make the decision to follow her dream when there was so much she would miss?

Aimee Boorman coached Simone for 11 years, from the time Simone entered her first gymnastics competition, until the 2016 Rio Olympics.

Required Learning

Simone's training involved learning the four required artistic gymnastics **apparatus** forms—balance beam, vault, uneven bars, and floor exercise. In competition, gymnasts are judged on the difficulty and execution of their routines. The gymnast with the highest score when all four results are calculated wins the all-around gold medal. Medals are also awarded to the highest-scoring athletes in each individual event.

A mistake in gymnastics such as a stumble, fall, awkward landing, or stepping outside a boundary line, leads to lower scores.

Balance Beam

Simone performs acrobatic and dance skills on a wooden beam that is 4 inches (10 cm) wide and 4 feet (1.2 m) above the ground. The routine lasts for 70 to 90 seconds and ends with a dismount.

Vault

On the vault, Simone runs fast and jumps off a springboard, vaulting onto a padded vaulting table. She lands on the other side on both feet.

Uneven Bars

Uneven bars are two bars above the ground, one high bar, and one lower. Simone performs a routine of swing-and-release moves going from one bar to the other, circling and twisting, and finishing with a dismount.

Floor Exercise

The floor exercise is a routine that includes acrobatic and dance moves, and is performed on a square springy floor.

Soaring

When Simone was 14 years old, she was **scouted** by the U.S. gymnastics team during her performance at the 2011 American Classic competition. She was asked by Márta Károlyi, the National Women's Gymnastics team coordinator, to join the team for some practices. In 2012, Simone won medals at four different national competitions, including the U.S. National Championships. She placed third there in the **all-around** category. After such amazing performances, Simone was named to the United States Junior National Team.

> " Simone brings a bubbly personality. In order to get to this level of gymnastics, not everything works out. Sometimes we have difficulty, but we have to push through. If you have a positive outlook, a bubbly personality like Simone, it is always a great contribution.
>
> —**Márta Károlyi, U.S. Women's Gymnastics Team Coordinator** "

Simone's cheerful and outgoing personality has won her many fans.

A Difficult Competition

A year after she burst onto the Junior National Team, however, things went all wrong. At the 2013 Secret Classic gymnastics event, Simone's nerves affected her focus. She hurt her ankle during a fall from the uneven bars, and stumbled on the balance beam. Anxious and worried that she might be injured, she pulled out of the vault competition altogether. It was a devastating and uncharacteristic performance, because Simone usually kept going through difficulty.

Mental Gymnastics

A sports psychologist helps athletes understand and improve how their thoughts and feelings contribute to their athletic performance.

Simone struggled to keep her emotions hidden about her performance at the 2013 Secret Classic in Chicago, Illinois.

A Winning Combination

Simone worked hard to prepare physically and mentally for the 2013 P&G Championship in Hartford, Connecticut. Her positive attitude and determination were back as she competed under pressure against Olympic champion, Kyla Ross. With technically difficult and near-perfect performances, Simone captured the all-around gold medal. She also won silver medals on the four apparatus events.

? THINK ABOUT IT

How did Simone's positive attitude help her deal with her nerves and compete under such pressure? What do you do to stay positive in a difficult situation?

Positivity in Motion

Simone's first international competition as a member of the U.S. World Championships Team took place in Antwerp, Belgium at the 2013 World Artistic Gymnastics Championships. Simone was 16 years old, and she felt strong both physically and mentally. She was the first American gymnast since Shannon Miller in 1991 to qualify in all four event finals, and the all-around final. She dominated in the finals, winning the all-around gold medal. Simone also won silver on vault, bronze on balance beam, and placed fourth on the uneven bars.

> One of my proudest moments was probably 2013 Worlds, because I proved to myself that I could do things that I didn't think I could.
>
> —Simone Biles, NBC interview

Simone's success at the P&G Championship was the beginning of a winning streak that took her skills to the international level. Here she is on the podium with fellow winners Kyla Ross (left) and Brenna Dowell (right).

The Pressure Is On

Despite a shoulder injury at the beginning of the season, Simone went on to win the U.S. and World titles in 2014. She returned to the Secret U.S. Classic that year, the same competition that had caused her to doubt her abilities in 2013. Simone wowed the crowd with a brand-new **signature move** during her floor exercise. She won gold in three events, as well as the all-around gold medal. With two world titles in hand, people began to think that she might be an **Olympic hopeful** for the 2016 Olympics in Rio, Brazil. But Simone still had work to do to earn a spot on the U.S. Olympic Team.

The Biles

In order to compete at the top level, she had to do something no one had seen before. The move she invented is a complicated double flip layout with a half-twist. It was named "The Biles" since Simone was the first person to do that combination of moves at a World Cup Event. Even though Simone thinks it's great to have a move named after her, she said she never thinks of it as "The Biles." To her, it's just a double layout with a half twist.

"The Biles"

Layout position
body is stretched out straight

Twist
A rotation of the body in mid-air

Taking a risk took courage, but it helped Simone become the champion that she is today.

All-Around Champion

Simone won the all-around gold medals at two world championships, and she felt pressure to win again. At the 2015 World Championships in Glasgow, Scotland, despite many mistakes, she won all-around gold once more. This made her the first woman to win three consecutive world titles in the all-around competition! Simone had a record 10 gold medals internationally, and 14 world championship medals in total—the most for a U.S. female gymnast. Yet even though she won the Worlds for the third time in a row and set new records, Simone was unhappy about her performance.

> **"**
>
> *I was pretty disappointed in how I did [at the 2015 Worlds in] Glasgow, because I knew I could do better.*
>
> — **Simone Biles, NBC interview**
>
> **"**

Believe It

Simone's dream of becoming an Olympic gymnast seemed within reach after she watched the American women's team compete in the 2012 London Olympics. Positive thinking helped Simone imagine herself as an Olympic athlete, and fueled her passion to make her dream come true.

Dare to Dream

Ron and Nellie Biles wanted to help Simone become the best she could be. They built a gymnastics training center in Spring, Texas, in 2016 so their daughter could train close to home in a world-class facility. They also wanted to encourage other gymnasts to follow their dreams. The World Champions Center offers programs from recreational gymnastics to competitive level training with specialized coaching and equipment.

Simone's parents and younger sister Adria proudly watch her at the 2016 Olympic Games in Brazil. Adria is also a skilled gymnast.

Team Player

On July 10, 2016, Simone's dream was realized. She earned a spot on the Olympic team after winning the all-around titles in the Pacific Rim International Championship and the USA Gymnastics Championship. In August 2016, she flew to Rio de Janeiro, Brazil, to represent her country along with her teammates, Aly Raisman, Gabby Douglas, Laurie Hernandez, and Madison Kocian. The team was known as "The Final Five," because it was the final time the Olympic games would have 5-member gymnastics teams instead of 4. Even though the girls were also competing individually, the gymnasts worked well as a team, cheering each other on.

> "Your teammates are one of the strongest support systems you can have whenever you go out to compete, because they help fill you with so much confidence. We all have this one goal, and we all put 100 percent effort into the same thing. I think that's really amazing."
>
> —Simone Biles

Success!

The Final Five dominated the Olympic podium, winning at least one medal in every event for a total of 14 medals. Simone won 5 medals — 4 gold, and 1 bronze. It was the most any American female gymnast has won in a single Olympics. As a final honor, the other American athletes voted for Simone to be the U.S. Olympic Team's **flag bearer** at the closing ceremony.

? THINK ABOUT IT

It can be difficult to cheer for your friends when you are trying to reach the same goal. What are some ways you encourage others when you play sports or work together at school? How does it help you achieve a goal when others encourage you?

Famous Five

Simone and her teammates in the Final Five were recognized in another significant way for their historic achievement at the Olympics in Rio. They were inducted into the USA Gymnastics Hall of Fame.

After celebrating the gold medal team victory at the 2016 Olympic Games, Simone tweeted "Dreams DO come true!"

After the Olympics, Simone was welcomed home to Spring, Texas, with a parade.

Life After Rio

Simone Biles arrived home to the United States a hero. No other American gymnast in history had ever won a combined 19 World and Olympic medals. She was a superstar! But the thrill of her success was overshadowed by a **computer hacker** who stole and leaked information about Simone's use of methylphenidate, or Ritalin. Simone's stolen medical records revealed that she has **Attention Deficit Hyperactivity Disorder (ADHD)**. The methylphenidate was a **medication** her doctor prescribed and she had received permission from Olympic officials to use it for her disorder. Simone spoke up about her use of Ritalin and not being ashamed of ADHD.

Telling Her Story

Simone partnered with journalist Michelle Burford to write a book about her life called *Courage to Soar: A Body in Motion, a Life in Balance.* She wanted to inspire people to have courage to get through tough times by sharing her own journey. In her book, Simone explains that to push yourself to make the most of your natural talents, you have to be willing to work hard, have fun, and always be brave.

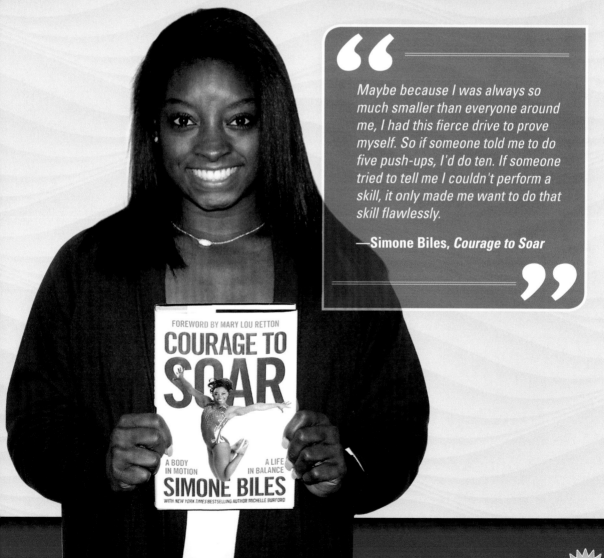

> **"**
> Maybe because I was always so much smaller than everyone around me, I had this fierce drive to prove myself. So if someone told me to do five push-ups, I'd do ten. If someone tried to tell me I couldn't perform a skill, it only made me want to do that skill flawlessly.
>
> —Simone Biles, *Courage to Soar*
> **"**

Role Model

With fame comes opportunity, and Simone has followed in the footsteps of other famous athletes by **endorsing** products, attending events, and speaking up publicly about things she believes in. Companies pay her to **promote** their products or services. They hope that people will want to buy them because they admire and trust Simone.

Standing Up

Simone supports causes that are close to her heart. She joined with other athletes to support Los Angeles, California's, bid to host an upcoming Summer Olympics. The bid was successful. In 2028, Los Angeles will host the Olympics, providing opportunities for athletes and lasting support to youth athletics programs in the future. Simone also supports athletes with **intellectual disabilities** by raising money for athletes to compete at the **Special Olympics**.

Simone feels strongly about endorsing products that promote a healthy lifestyle.

Bravely Coming Forward

In 2018, Simone stood up for team members and others who were assaulted by a team doctor, Larry Nassar. He was charged, convicted, and sentenced to 40 to 175 years in prison for his sexual abuse. Simone also bravely came forward to say that she also, had been sexually abused by Nassar. Simone applauded the sentence and told fellow survivors that he "will no longer have the power to steal our happiness or joy."

Simone remembers being hungry in her early years. She now supports nokidhungry.org in ending child hunger.

Talking the Talk, Walking the Walk

Helping young people be physically and mentally healthy is one of Simone's passions. She speaks to kids about the benefits of eating well and being active so they can continue living healthy lifestyles as adults. Simone is also an **ambassador** for the Ask, Listen, Learn program that helps young people understand the dangers of alcohol and the importance of living a healthy lifestyle. She makes public service announcements (PSAs) for the Foundation for Advancing Alcohol Responsibility. This is an organization that educates people on the abuse of alcohol and encourages youth to not drink underage.

Putting on Her Dancing Shoes

Having fun and trying something new are also things Simone Biles loves. In 2017, she was a contestant on *Dancing with the Stars*, a television show that pairs professional ballroom dancers with **celebrities** in a dance competition. Simone and professional dancer, Sasha Farber, made it to the semi-finals. On one show, Simone chose to honor her parents by telling her life story through a Viennese Waltz. When the music ended, Simone ran over to the audience to hug both of her parents who were in tears after her touching performance. Simone and Sasha did not win the competition, but they did earn two perfect scores for their dance.

My parents saved me. They've set huge examples of how to treat other people and they've been there to support me since day one. There's nothing I can say to them to thank them enough. Even though there's no right words, maybe dance will say it for me.

— Simone Biles,
Dancing with the Stars

Simone shared her respect and love for her parents in a dance.

Hometown Help

Simone and her family feel strongly about helping people in need. After devastating floods destroyed many homes in parts of Texas during Hurricane Harvey in August 2017, Simone was eager to lend a hand. Simone's home was not affected, even though her hometown, a suburb of Houston, was hit very hard. She and her family and friends volunteered their time in a **distribution center**. They sorted and handed out clothes to those who had lost everything in the flood caused by the hurricane.

? THINK ABOUT IT

Simone is grateful for the support she has received throughout the years. One way she gives back is by volunteering. Can you think of a way you can help people in your community, country, or the world?

More than 10,000 people found shelter in the Houston Convention Center during Hurricane Harvey.

Reaching New Heights

Simone has won numerous awards for her incredible athleticism, including Team USA's Female Olympic Athlete of the Year Award in 2015, Nickelodeon's 2017 Kids' Choice Favorite Female Athlete Award, and the ESPY Award for Best Female Athlete of 2017. Young people look up to her for her dedication to sport, her fun-loving personality, and her courage. Simone's journey hasn't always been easy, but she never gave up on herself or her dreams. With a strong, loving family, the support of her coach, and a positive attitude, Simone is a true champion!

> *I'm not alone; my family is with me when I'm out there competing. And I do believe in myself. I really do.*
>
> — **Simone Biles, CNN.com**

Writing Prompts

1. What are some ways you are similar to Simone? How are you different? If you were a famous person, what would you be famous for? A sport? An invention? How would your life change?

2. Simone Biles works hard to stay in top form as an Olympic athlete. She has a positive attitude, and she presses on through difficulty. What can you do to stay focused with a positive attitude to achieve your dreams? Write down your goals and go for it!

3. Simone believes in making healthy lifestyle choices. What are some healthy habits you have? What could you do to be even more healthy?

Learning More

Books

Courage to Soar: A Body in Motion, A Life in Balance by Simone Biles and Michelle Burford. Zondervan Publishing, 2016.

Simone Biles, Superstar of Gymnastics (GymnStars) by Christine Dzidrums. Creative Media Publishing. 2016.

Simone Biles (Sports All-Stars) by Jon Fishman. Lerner Publishing, 2016.

Websites

www.simonebiles.com
Simone's official website includes photographs, lists of awards and medals, a short biography, sponsors, and a free chapter from her book.

www.olympic.org
Check out the Olympics online! Access videos of past Olympics (including Rio 2016), read about the venues, and check out the stats.

www.dkfindout.com/us/sports/gymnastics/
This web page gives a brief explanation of different types of gymnastics. It also has an interactive photo explaining the requirements for the costume, hair, bare feet, and equipment used.

Glossary

Please note: Some bold-faced words are defined where they appear in the text.

all-around The use of all of the different gymnastics apparatuses

ambassador A person who represents a product, company, or organization

apparatus The equipment needed to perform particular moves in gymnastics

Attention Deficit Hyperactivity Disorder (ADHD) A condition in which the brain experiences a pattern of inattention, or hyperactive impulses, or both

celebrities People who are famous and easily recognized in the media

computer hacker Someone who secretly gets into a computer system to access private information or cause damage

distribution center A place where donations of clothing and food are taken in, sorted, and distributed to people in need

endorsing Publicly declaring one's support or approval of something

flag bearer Someone who carries the flag for their country during a public event, such as the Olympics

foster care A system of services that include providing a temporary home for children who are unable to live with their own parents

homeschooled Being taught at home by a parent or caregiver

intellectual disabilities Limited problem-solving and reasoning skills that affect a person's daily life

medication A drug prescribed by a medical doctor

Olympic hopeful An athlete that has a strong chance of making it to the Olympics

perseverance Continuing to try to do or achieve something even when it is difficult

positivity Having a good attitude in all situations

promote To support or actively encourage

scouted Considered for a position on a team

signature move A move that is attributed to a specific person and for which that person is known

Special Olympics An international competition in which intellectually and physically challenged athletes compete

Index